S0-BXW-450

Disney's
Wonderful World of Reading®

Your child will love storybooks based on favorite Disney movies

Spending story time with favorite Disney friends is one of the unforgettable joys of being a child. And now all the lovable characters that won your child's heart in the movies are waiting to come to life in colorful storybooks that fill young imaginations with fun!

Disney storybooks are filled with timeless adventures … fantastic Disney artwork … eye-popping spectacle … and laugh-a-minute fun. Your child will read each fun-filled story over and over again. What a wonderful way to teach your child to love books and reading!

Go ahead. Return one of the attached order cards to get eight Disney storybooks for just $3.99, plus shipping and handling. It's an incredible value you won't want to miss.

Return a reply card today to get 8 storybooks for just $3.99!

Plus shipping and handling.

Plus a FREE Backpack!

© Disney/Pixar

Book titles subject to change.

DETACH HERE AND MAIL TODAY

☐ YES! I want my child to have 8 great Disney storybooks for only $3.99*!

Please accept my request and send the eight books shown plus the FREE Backpack and bill me for only $3.99*.

If not completely satisfied, I may return the books at Scholastic's expense within seven days and owe Scholastic nothing.

As a member, I will receive two books about every four weeks on seven-day approval for only $4.99* per book.

I may examine every book FREE for seven days and return any at Scholastic's expense. After accepting as few as four shipments of two books each, I may cancel at any time by following the instructions on my invoice.

By joining, each year I will also receive, on approval, a Disney Yearbook, Disney Calendar and a third Disney item. I will be notified prior to each shipment with details and the price; I may cancel any shipment I do not wish to receive.

The FREE Backpack is mine to keep even if I purchase nothing.

Print Child's Full Name ______________________

Birthdate: Month ________ Day ________ Year ________ ☐ Boy ☐ Girl

Address ______________________ Apt. ________

City ______________ State ________ Zip ________

Print Your Full Name ☐ Mr. ☐ Ms. ☐ Mrs. ______________________

Phone (Area Code________)______________________

E-mail______________________

Have you bought anything by mail in the last: ☐ 6 months ☐ Year ☐ Never

Do you own a computer? ☐ Yes ☐ No

CODE: 376402RVG-7

* Plus shipping, handling and applicable sales tax. Late charges apply to overdue payments. All orders subject to approval. Out-of-stock titles may be replaced by alternate selections.

DBC-DR104

If cards are missing, write to:

SCHOLASTIC
2931 EAST McCARTY STREET
JEFFERSON CITY, MO 65101

DETACH HERE AND MAIL TODAY

☐ YES! I want my child to have 8 great Disney storybooks for only $3.99*!

Please accept my request and send the eight books shown plus the FREE Backpack and bill me for only $3.99*.

If not completely satisfied, I may return the books at Scholastic's expense within seven days and owe Scholastic nothing.

As a member, I will receive two books about every four weeks on seven-day approval for only $4.99* per book.

I may examine every book FREE for seven days and return any at Scholastic's expense. After accepting as few as four shipments of two books each, I may cancel at any time by following the instructions on my invoice.

By joining, each year I will also receive, on approval, a Disney Yearbook, Disney Calendar and a third Disney item. I will be notified prior to each shipment with details and the price; I may cancel any shipment I do not wish to receive.

The FREE Backpack is mine to keep even if I purchase nothing.

Print Child's Full Name ______________________

Birthdate: Month ________ Day ________ Year ________ ☐ Boy ☐ Girl

Address ______________________ Apt. ________

City ______________ State ________ Zip ________

Print Your Full Name ☐ Mr. ☐ Ms. ☐ Mrs. ______________________

Phone (Area Code________)______________________

E-mail______________________

Have you bought anything by mail in the last: ☐ 6 months ☐ Year ☐ Never

Do you own a computer? ☐ Yes ☐ No

CODE: 376402RVG-7

* Plus shipping, handling and applicable sales tax. Late charges apply to overdue payments. All orders subject to approval. Out-of-stock titles may be replaced by alternate selections.

DBC-DR104

© Disney

NO POSTAGE NECESSARY IF MAILED IN THE UNITED STATES

BUSINESS REPLY MAIL

FIRST-CLASS MAIL PERMIT NO. 48 JEFFERSON CITY, MO

POSTAGE WILL BE PAID BY ADDRESSEE

SCHOLASTIC
PO BOX 6114
JEFFERSON CITY MO 65102-9670

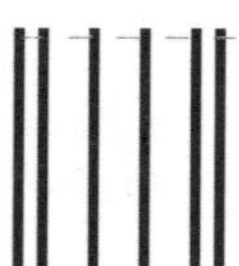

NO POSTAGE NECESSARY IF MAILED IN THE UNITED STATES

BUSINESS REPLY MAIL

FIRST-CLASS MAIL PERMIT NO. 48 JEFFERSON CITY, MO

POSTAGE WILL BE PAID BY ADDRESSEE

SCHOLASTIC
PO BOX 6114
JEFFERSON CITY MO 65102-9670

DETACH HERE AND MAIL TODAY

☐ YES! I want my child to have 8 great Disney storybooks for only $3.99*!

Please accept my request and send the eight books shown plus the FREE Backpack and bill me for only $3.99*.

If not completely satisfied, I may return the books at Scholastic's expense within seven days and owe Scholastic nothing.

As a member, I will receive two books about every four weeks on seven-day approval for only $4.99* per book.

I may examine every book FREE for seven days and return any at Scholastic's expense. After accepting as few as four shipments of two books each, I may cancel at any time by following the instructions on my invoice.

By joining, each year I will also receive, on approval, a Disney Yearbook, Disney Calendar and a third Disney item. I will be notified prior to each shipment with details and the price; I may cancel any shipment I do not wish to receive.

The FREE Backpack is mine to keep even if I purchase nothing.

Print Child's Full Name ____________________

Birthdate: Month ____________ Day ____________ Year ____________ ☐ Boy ☐ Girl

Address ____________________ Apt. ____________

City ____________________ State ____________ Zip ____________

Print Your Full Name ☐ Mr. ☐ Ms. ☐ Mrs. ____________________

Phone (Area Code ____________) ____________________

E-mail ____________________

Have you bought anything by mail in the last: ☐ 6 months ☐ Year ☐ Never

Do you own a computer? ☐ Yes ☐ No

CODE: 376402RVG-7

* Plus shipping, handling and applicable sales tax. Late charges apply to overdue payments. All orders subject to approval. Out-of-stock titles may be replaced by alternate selections.

DBC-DR104

© Disney

If cards are missing, write to:

SCHOLASTIC
2931 EAST McCARTY STREET
JEFFERSON CITY, MO 65101

© Disney

DETACH HERE AND MAIL TODAY

☐ YES! I want my child to have 8 great Disney storybooks for only $3.99*!

Please accept my request and send the eight books shown plus the FREE Backpack and bill me for only $3.99*.

If not completely satisfied, I may return the books at Scholastic's expense within seven days and owe Scholastic nothing.

As a member, I will receive two books about every four weeks on seven-day approval for only $4.99* per book.

I may examine every book FREE for seven days and return any at Scholastic's expense. After accepting as few as four shipments of two books each, I may cancel at any time by following the instructions on my invoice.

By joining, each year I will also receive, on approval, a Disney Yearbook, Disney Calendar and a third Disney item. I will be notified prior to each shipment with details and the price; I may cancel any shipment I do not wish to receive.

The FREE Backpack is mine to keep even if I purchase nothing.

Print Child's Full Name ____________________

Birthdate: Month ____________ Day ____________ Year ____________ ☐ Boy ☐ Girl

Address ____________________ Apt. ____________

City ____________________ State ____________ Zip ____________

Print Your Full Name ☐ Mr. ☐ Ms. ☐ Mrs. ____________________

Phone (Area Code ____________) ____________________

E-mail ____________________

Have you bought anything by mail in the last: ☐ 6 months ☐ Year ☐ Never

Do you own a computer? ☐ Yes ☐ No

CODE: 376402RVG-7

* Plus shipping, handling and applicable sales tax. Late charges apply to overdue payments. All orders subject to approval. Out-of-stock titles may be replaced by alternate selections.

DBC-DR104

© Disney

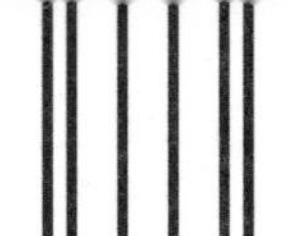

NO POSTAGE
NECESSARY IF
MAILED IN THE
UNITED STATES

BUSINESS REPLY MAIL

FIRST-CLASS MAIL PERMIT NO. 48 JEFFERSON CITY, MO

POSTAGE WILL BE PAID BY ADDRESSEE

SCHOLASTIC
PO BOX 6114
JEFFERSON CITY MO 65102-9670

NO POSTAGE
NECESSARY IF
MAILED IN THE
UNITED STATES

BUSINESS REPLY MAIL

FIRST-CLASS MAIL PERMIT NO. 48 JEFFERSON CITY, MO

POSTAGE WILL BE PAID BY ADDRESSEE

SCHOLASTIC
PO BOX 6114
JEFFERSON CITY MO 65102-9670

DETACH HERE AND MAIL TODAY

☐ YES! I want my child to have 8 great Disney storybooks for only $3.99*!

Please accept my request and send the eight books shown plus the FREE Backpack and bill me for only $3.99*.

If not completely satisfied, I may return the books at Scholastic's expense within seven days and owe Scholastic nothing.

As a member, I will receive two books about every four weeks on seven-day approval for only $4.99* per book.

I may examine every book FREE for seven days and return any at Scholastic's expense. After accepting as few as four shipments of two books each, I may cancel at any time by following the instructions on my invoice.

By joining, each year I will also receive, on approval, a Disney Yearbook, Disney Calendar and a third Disney item. I will be notified prior to each shipment with details and the price; I may cancel any shipment I do not wish to receive.

The FREE Backpack is mine to keep even if I purchase nothing.

Print Child's Full Name ______________________

Birthdate: Month __________ Day __________ Year __________ ☐ Boy ☐ Girl

Address ______________________ Apt. __________

City ______________________ State __________ Zip __________

Print Your Full Name ☐ Mr. ☐ Ms. ☐ Mrs. ______________________

Phone (Area Code__________)______________________

E-mail ______________________

Have you bought anything by mail in the last: ☐ 6 months ☐ Year ☐ Never

Do you own a computer? ☐ Yes ☐ No

CODE: 376402RVG-7

* Plus shipping, handling and applicable sales tax. Late charges apply to overdue payments. All orders subject to approval. Out-of-stock titles may be replaced by alternate selections.

DBC-DR104

© Disney

If cards are missing, write to:

SCHOLASTIC
2931 EAST McCARTY STREET
JEFFERSON CITY, MO 65101

© Disney

DETACH HERE AND MAIL TODAY

☐ YES! I want my child to have 8 great Disney storybooks for only $3.99*!

Please accept my request and send the eight books shown plus the FREE Backpack and bill me for only $3.99*.

If not completely satisfied, I may return the books at Scholastic's expense within seven days and owe Scholastic nothing.

As a member, I will receive two books about every four weeks on seven-day approval for only $4.99* per book.

I may examine every book FREE for seven days and return any at Scholastic's expense. After accepting as few as four shipments of two books each, I may cancel at any time by following the instructions on my invoice.

By joining, each year I will also receive, on approval, a Disney Yearbook, Disney Calendar and a third Disney item. I will be notified prior to each shipment with details and the price; I may cancel any shipment I do not wish to receive.

The FREE Backpack is mine to keep even if I purchase nothing.

Print Child's Full Name ______________________

Birthdate: Month __________ Day __________ Year __________ ☐ Boy ☐ Girl

Address ______________________ Apt. __________

City ______________________ State __________ Zip __________

Print Your Full Name ☐ Mr. ☐ Ms. ☐ Mrs. ______________________

Phone (Area Code__________)______________________

E-mail ______________________

Have you bought anything by mail in the last: ☐ 6 months ☐ Year ☐ Never

Do you own a computer? ☐ Yes ☐ No

CODE: 376402RVG-7

* Plus shipping, handling and applicable sales tax. Late charges apply to overdue payments. All orders subject to approval. Out-of-stock titles may be replaced by alternate selections.

DBC-DR104

© Disney

NO POSTAGE
NECESSARY IF
MAILED IN THE
UNITED STATES

BUSINESS REPLY MAIL

FIRST-CLASS MAIL PERMIT NO. 48 JEFFERSON CITY, MO

POSTAGE WILL BE PAID BY ADDRESSEE

SCHOLASTIC
PO BOX 6114
JEFFERSON CITY MO 65102-9670

NO POSTAGE
NECESSARY IF
MAILED IN THE
UNITED STATES

BUSINESS REPLY MAIL

FIRST-CLASS MAIL PERMIT NO. 48 JEFFERSON CITY, MO

POSTAGE WILL BE PAID BY ADDRESSEE

SCHOLASTIC
PO BOX 6114
JEFFERSON CITY MO 65102-9670

DETACH HERE AND MAIL TODAY

☐ YES! I want my child to have 8 great Disney storybooks for only $3.99*!

Please accept my request and send the eight books shown plus the FREE Backpack and bill me for only $3.99*.
If not completely satisfied, I may return the books at Scholastic's expense within seven days and owe Scholastic nothing.
As a member, I will receive two books about every four weeks on seven-day approval for only $4.99* per book.

I may examine every book FREE for seven days and return any at Scholastic's expense. After accepting as few as four shipments of two books each, I may cancel at any time by following the instructions on my invoice.

By joining, each year I will also receive, on approval, a Disney Yearbook, Disney Calendar and a third Disney item. I will be notified prior to each shipment with details and the price; I may cancel any shipment I do not wish to receive.

The FREE Backpack is mine to keep even if I purchase nothing.

Print Child's Full Name ______________________________

Birthdate: Month ____________ Day ____________ Year ____________ ☐ Boy ☐ Girl

Address ______________________________ Apt. ____________

City ______________________ State ____________ Zip ____________

Print Your Full Name ☐ Mr. ☐ Ms. ☐ Mrs. ______________________________

Phone (Area Code__________)______________________________

E-mail ______________________________

Have you bought anything by mail in the last: ☐ 6 months ☐ Year ☐ Never

Do you own a computer? ☐ Yes ☐ No

CODE: 376402RVG-7

* Plus shipping, handling and applicable sales tax. Late charges apply to overdue payments. All orders subject to approval. Out-of-stock titles may be replaced by alternate selections.

DBC-DR104

If cards are missing, write to:

SCHOLASTIC
2931 EAST McCARTY STREET
JEFFERSON CITY, MO 65101

DETACH HERE AND MAIL TODAY

☐ YES! I want my child to have 8 great Disney storybooks for only $3.99*!

Please accept my request and send the eight books shown plus the FREE Backpack and bill me for only $3.99*.
If not completely satisfied, I may return the books at Scholastic's expense within seven days and owe Scholastic nothing.
As a member, I will receive two books about every four weeks on seven-day approval for only $4.99* per book.

I may examine every book FREE for seven days and return any at Scholastic's expense. After accepting as few as four shipments of two books each, I may cancel at any time by following the instructions on my invoice.

By joining, each year I will also receive, on approval, a Disney Yearbook, Disney Calendar and a third Disney item. I will be notified prior to each shipment with details and the price; I may cancel any shipment I do not wish to receive.

The FREE Backpack is mine to keep even if I purchase nothing.

Print Child's Full Name ______________________________

Birthdate: Month ____________ Day ____________ Year ____________ ☐ Boy ☐ Girl

Address ______________________________ Apt. ____________

City ______________________ State ____________ Zip ____________

Print Your Full Name ☐ Mr. ☐ Ms. ☐ Mrs. ______________________________

Phone (Area Code__________)______________________________

E-mail ______________________________

Have you bought anything by mail in the last: ☐ 6 months ☐ Year ☐ Never

Do you own a computer? ☐ Yes ☐ No

CODE: 376402RVG-7

* Plus shipping, handling and applicable sales tax. Late charges apply to overdue payments. All orders subject to approval. Out-of-stock titles may be replaced by alternate selections.

DBC-DR104

© Disney

NO POSTAGE NECESSARY IF MAILED IN THE UNITED STATES

BUSINESS REPLY MAIL

FIRST-CLASS MAIL PERMIT NO. 48 JEFFERSON CITY, MO

POSTAGE WILL BE PAID BY ADDRESSEE

SCHOLASTIC
PO BOX 6114
JEFFERSON CITY MO 65102-9670

NO POSTAGE NECESSARY IF MAILED IN THE UNITED STATES

BUSINESS REPLY MAIL

FIRST-CLASS MAIL PERMIT NO. 48 JEFFERSON CITY, MO

POSTAGE WILL BE PAID BY ADDRESSEE

SCHOLASTIC
PO BOX 6114
JEFFERSON CITY MO 65102-9670

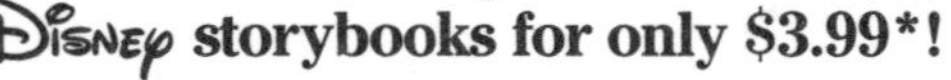

☐ YES! I want my child to have 8 great

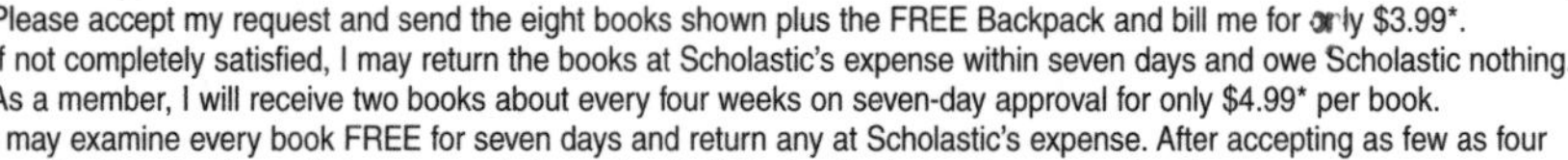

Disney storybooks for only $3.99*!

Please accept my request and send the eight books shown plus the FREE Backpack and bill me for only $3.99*.
If not completely satisfied, I may return the books at Scholastic's expense within seven days and owe Scholastic nothing.
As a member, I will receive two books about every four weeks on seven-day approval for only $4.99* per book.
I may examine every book FREE for seven days and return any at Scholastic's expense. After accepting as few as four shipments of two books each, I may cancel at any time by following the instructions on my invoice.
By joining, each year I will also receive, on approval, a Disney Yearbook, Disney Calendar and a third Disney item. I will be notified prior to each shipment with details and the price; I may cancel any shipment I do not wish to receive.
The FREE Backpack is mine to keep even if I purchase nothing.

Print Child's Full Name ______________________

Birthdate: Month ________ Day ________ Year ________ ☐ Boy ☐ Girl

Address ______________________ Apt. ________

City ______________ State ________ Zip ________

Print Your Full Name ☐ Mr. ☐ Ms. ☐ Mrs. ______________________

Phone (Area Code________)______________________

E-mail______________________

Have you bought anything by mail in the last: ☐ 6 months ☐ Year ☐ Never

Do you own a computer? ☐ Yes ☐ No

CODE: 376402RVG-7

* Plus shipping, handling and applicable sales tax. Late charges apply to overdue payments. All orders subject to approval. Out-of-stock titles may be replaced by alternate selections.

DBC-DR104

If cards are missing, write to:

SCHOLASTIC
2931 EAST McCARTY STREET
JEFFERSON CITY, MO 65101

☐ YES! I want my child to have 8 great
Disney storybooks for only $3.99*!

Please accept my request and send the eight books shown plus the FREE Backpack and bill me for only $3.99*.
If not completely satisfied, I may return the books at Scholastic's expense within seven days and owe Scholastic nothing.
As a member, I will receive two books about every four weeks on seven-day approval for only $4.99* per book.
I may examine every book FREE for seven days and return any at Scholastic's expense. After accepting as few as four shipments of two books each, I may cancel at any time by following the instructions on my invoice.
By joining, each year I will also receive, on approval, a Disney Yearbook, Disney Calendar and a third Disney item. I will be notified prior to each shipment with details and the price; I may cancel any shipment I do not wish to receive.
The FREE Backpack is mine to keep even if I purchase nothing.

Print Child's Full Name ______________________

Birthdate: Month ________ Day ________ Year ________ ☐ Boy ☐ Girl

Address ______________________ Apt. ________

City ______________ State ________ Zip ________

Print Your Full Name ☐ Mr. ☐ Ms. ☐ Mrs. ______________________

Phone (Area Code________)______________________

E-mail______________________

Have you bought anything by mail in the last: ☐ 6 months ☐ Year ☐ Never

Do you own a computer? ☐ Yes ☐ No

CODE: 376402RVG-7

* Plus shipping, handling and applicable sales tax. Late charges apply to overdue payments. All orders subject to approval. Out-of-stock titles may be replaced by alternate selections.

DBC-DR104

© Disney

NO POSTAGE
NECESSARY IF
MAILED IN THE
UNITED STATES

BUSINESS REPLY MAIL

FIRST-CLASS MAIL PERMIT NO. 48 JEFFERSON CITY, MO

POSTAGE WILL BE PAID BY ADDRESSEE

SCHOLASTIC
PO BOX 6114
JEFFERSON CITY MO 65102-9670

NO POSTAGE
NECESSARY IF
MAILED IN THE
UNITED STATES

BUSINESS REPLY MAIL

FIRST-CLASS MAIL PERMIT NO. 48 JEFFERSON CITY, MO

POSTAGE WILL BE PAID BY ADDRESSEE

SCHOLASTIC
PO BOX 6114
JEFFERSON CITY MO 65102-9670

DETACH HERE AND MAIL TODAY

☐ YES! I want my child to have 8 great Disney storybooks for only $3.99*!

Please accept my request and send the eight books shown plus the FREE Backpack and bill me for only $3.99*. If not completely satisfied, I may return the books at Scholastic's expense within seven days and owe Scholastic nothing. As a member, I will receive two books about every four weeks on seven-day approval for only $4.99* per book.

I may examine every book FREE for seven days and return any at Scholastic's expense. After accepting as few as four shipments of two books each, I may cancel at any time by following the instructions on my invoice.

By joining, each year I will also receive, on approval, a Disney Yearbook, Disney Calendar and a third Disney item. I will be notified prior to each shipment with details and the price; I may cancel any shipment I do not wish to receive.

The FREE Backpack is mine to keep even if I purchase nothing.

Print Child's Full Name ______________________

Birthdate: Month ____________ Day ____________ Year ____________ ☐ Boy ☐ Girl

Address ______________________ Apt. ________

City ______________________ State ________ Zip ________

Print Your Full Name ☐ Mr. ☐ Ms. ☐ Mrs. ______________________

Phone (Area Code ________) ______________________

E-mail ______________________

Have you bought anything by mail in the last: ☐ 6 months ☐ Year ☐ Never

Do you own a computer? ☐ Yes ☐ No

CODE: 376402RVG-7

* Plus shipping, handling and applicable sales tax. Late charges apply to overdue payments. All orders subject to approval. Out-of-stock titles may be replaced by alternate selections.

DBC-DR104

If cards are missing, write to:

SCHOLASTIC
2931 EAST McCARTY STREET
JEFFERSON CITY, MO 65101

DETACH HERE AND MAIL TODAY

☐ YES! I want my child to have 8 great Disney storybooks for only $3.99*!

Please accept my request and send the eight books shown plus the FREE Backpack and bill me for only $3.99*. If not completely satisfied, I may return the books at Scholastic's expense within seven days and owe Scholastic nothing. As a member, I will receive two books about every four weeks on seven-day approval for only $4.99* per book.

I may examine every book FREE for seven days and return any at Scholastic's expense. After accepting as few as four shipments of two books each, I may cancel at any time by following the instructions on my invoice.

By joining, each year I will also receive, on approval, a Disney Yearbook, Disney Calendar and a third Disney item. I will be notified prior to each shipment with details and the price; I may cancel any shipment I do not wish to receive.

The FREE Backpack is mine to keep even if I purchase nothing.

Print Child's Full Name ______________________

Birthdate: Month ____________ Day ____________ Year ____________ ☐ Boy ☐ Girl

Address ______________________ Apt. ________

City ______________________ State ________ Zip ________

Print Your Full Name ☐ Mr. ☐ Ms. ☐ Mrs. ______________________

Phone (Area Code ________) ______________________

E-mail ______________________

Have you bought anything by mail in the last: ☐ 6 months ☐ Year ☐ Never

Do you own a computer? ☐ Yes ☐ No

CODE: 376402RVG-7

* Plus shipping, handling and applicable sales tax. Late charges apply to overdue payments. All orders subject to approval. Out-of-stock titles may be replaced by alternate selections.

DBC-DR104

© Disney

NO POSTAGE NECESSARY IF MAILED IN THE UNITED STATES

BUSINESS REPLY MAIL

FIRST-CLASS MAIL PERMIT NO. 48 JEFFERSON CITY, MO

POSTAGE WILL BE PAID BY ADDRESSEE

SCHOLASTIC
PO BOX 6114
JEFFERSON CITY MO 65102-9670

NO POSTAGE NECESSARY IF MAILED IN THE UNITED STATES

BUSINESS REPLY MAIL

FIRST-CLASS MAIL PERMIT NO. 48 JEFFERSON CITY, MO

POSTAGE WILL BE PAID BY ADDRESSEE

SCHOLASTIC
PO BOX 6114
JEFFERSON CITY MO 65102-9670

DETACH HERE AND MAIL TODAY

☐ YES! I want my child to have 8 great Disney storybooks for only $3.99*!

Please accept my request and send the eight books shown plus the FREE Backpack and bill me for only $3.99*.

If not completely satisfied, I may return the books at Scholastic's expense within seven days and owe Scholastic nothing.

As a member, I will receive two books about every four weeks on seven-day approval for only $4.99* per book.

I may examine every book FREE for seven days and return any at Scholastic's expense. After accepting as few as four shipments of two books each, I may cancel at any time by following the instructions on my invoice.

By joining, each year I will also receive, on approval, a Disney Yearbook, Disney Calendar and a third Disney item. I will be notified prior to each shipment with details and the price; I may cancel any shipment I do not wish to receive.

The FREE Backpack is mine to keep even if I purchase nothing.

Print Child's Full Name ______________________

Birthdate: Month __________ Day __________ Year __________ ☐ Boy ☐ Girl

Address ______________________ Apt. __________

City ______________________ State __________ Zip __________

Print Your Full Name ☐ Mr. ☐ Ms. ☐ Mrs. ______________________

Phone (Area Code__________)______________________

E-mail ______________________

Have you bought anything by mail in the last: ☐ 6 months ☐ Year ☐ Never

Do you own a computer? ☐ Yes ☐ No

CODE: 376402RVG-7

* Plus shipping, handling and applicable sales tax. Late charges apply to overdue payments. All orders subject to approval. Out-of-stock titles may be replaced by alternate selections.

DBC-DR104

If cards are missing, write to:

SCHOLASTIC
2931 EAST McCARTY STREET
JEFFERSON CITY, MO 65101

DETACH HERE AND MAIL TODAY

☐ YES! I want my child to have 8 great Disney storybooks for only $3.99*!

Please accept my request and send the eight books shown plus the FREE Backpack and bill me for only $3.99*.

If not completely satisfied, I may return the books at Scholastic's expense within seven days and owe Scholastic nothing.

As a member, I will receive two books about every four weeks on seven-day approval for only $4.99* per book.

I may examine every book FREE for seven days and return any at Scholastic's expense. After accepting as few as four shipments of two books each, I may cancel at any time by following the instructions on my invoice.

By joining, each year I will also receive, on approval, a Disney Yearbook, Disney Calendar and a third Disney item. I will be notified prior to each shipment with details and the price; I may cancel any shipment I do not wish to receive.

The FREE Backpack is mine to keep even if I purchase nothing.

Print Child's Full Name ______________________

Birthdate: Month __________ Day __________ Year __________ ☐ Boy ☐ Girl

Address ______________________ Apt. __________

City ______________________ State __________ Zip __________

Print Your Full Name ☐ Mr. ☐ Ms. ☐ Mrs. ______________________

Phone (Area Code__________)______________________

E-mail ______________________

Have you bought anything by mail in the last: ☐ 6 months ☐ Year ☐ Never

Do you own a computer? ☐ Yes ☐ No

CODE: 376402RVG-7

* Plus shipping, handling and applicable sales tax. Late charges apply to overdue payments. All orders subject to approval. Out-of-stock titles may be replaced by alternate selections.

DBC-DR104

© Disney

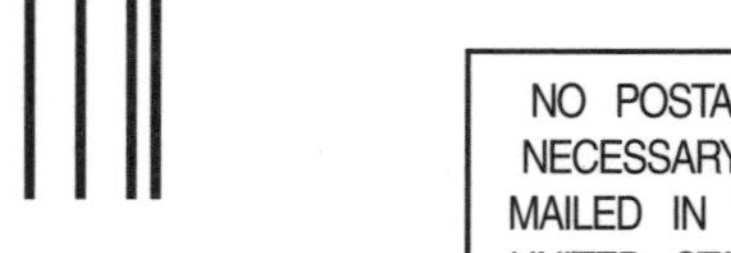

NO POSTAGE NECESSARY IF MAILED IN THE UNITED STATES

BUSINESS REPLY MAIL

FIRST-CLASS MAIL PERMIT NO. 48 JEFFERSON CITY, MO

POSTAGE WILL BE PAID BY ADDRESSEE

SCHOLASTIC
PO BOX 6114
JEFFERSON CITY MO 65102-9670

NO POSTAGE NECESSARY IF MAILED IN THE UNITED STATES

BUSINESS REPLY MAIL

FIRST-CLASS MAIL PERMIT NO. 48 JEFFERSON CITY, MO

POSTAGE WILL BE PAID BY ADDRESSEE

SCHOLASTIC
PO BOX 6114
JEFFERSON CITY MO 65102-9670

DETACH HERE AND MAIL TODAY

☐ YES! I want my child to have 8 great Disney storybooks for only $3.99*!

Please accept my request and send the eight books shown plus the FREE Backpack and bill me for only $3.99*.

If not completely satisfied, I may return the books at Scholastic's expense within seven days and owe Scholastic nothing.

As a member, I will receive two books about every four weeks on seven-day approval for only $4.99* per book.

I may examine every book FREE for seven days and return any at Scholastic's expense. After accepting as few as four shipments of two books each, I may cancel at any time by following the instructions on my invoice.

By joining, each year I will also receive, on approval, a Disney Yearbook, Disney Calendar and a third Disney item. I will be notified prior to each shipment with details and the price; I may cancel any shipment I do not wish to receive.

The FREE Backpack is mine to keep even if I purchase nothing.

Print Child's Full Name ______________________________

Birthdate: Month ____________ Day ____________ Year ____________ ☐ Boy ☐ Girl

Address ______________________________ Apt. ____________

City ____________________ State ____________ Zip ____________

Print Your Full Name ☐ Mr. ☐ Ms. ☐ Mrs. ______________________________

Phone (Area Code ________) ______________________________

E-mail ______________________________

Have you bought anything by mail in the last: ☐ 6 months ☐ Year ☐ Never

Do you own a computer? ☐ Yes ☐ No

CODE: 376402RVG-7

* Plus shipping, handling and applicable sales tax. Late charges apply to overdue payments. All orders subject to approval. Out-of-stock titles may be replaced by alternate selections.

DBC-DR104

If cards are missing, write to:

SCHOLASTIC
2931 EAST McCARTY STREET
JEFFERSON CITY, MO 65101

DETACH HERE AND MAIL TODAY

☐ YES! I want my child to have 8 great Disney storybooks for only $3.99*!

Please accept my request and send the eight books shown plus the FREE Backpack and bill me for only $3.99*.

If not completely satisfied, I may return the books at Scholastic's expense within seven days and owe Scholastic nothing.

As a member, I will receive two books about every four weeks on seven-day approval for only $4.99* per book.

I may examine every book FREE for seven days and return any at Scholastic's expense. After accepting as few as four shipments of two books each, I may cancel at any time by following the instructions on my invoice.

By joining, each year I will also receive, on approval, a Disney Yearbook, Disney Calendar and a third Disney item. I will be notified prior to each shipment with details and the price; I may cancel any shipment I do not wish to receive.

The FREE Backpack is mine to keep even if I purchase nothing.

Print Child's Full Name ______________________________

Birthdate: Month ____________ Day ____________ Year ____________ ☐ Boy ☐ Girl

Address ______________________________ Apt. ____________

City ____________________ State ____________ Zip ____________

Print Your Full Name ☐ Mr. ☐ Ms. ☐ Mrs. ______________________________

Phone (Area Code ________) ______________________________

E-mail ______________________________

Have you bought anything by mail in the last: ☐ 6 months ☐ Year ☐ Never

Do you own a computer? ☐ Yes ☐ No

CODE: 376402RVG-7

* Plus shipping, handling and applicable sales tax. Late charges apply to overdue payments. All orders subject to approval. Out-of-stock titles may be replaced by alternate selections.

DBC-DR104

© Disney

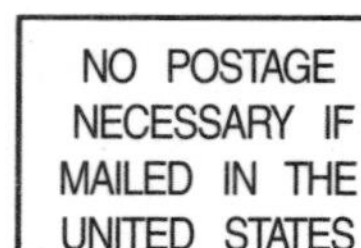

BUSINESS REPLY MAIL

FIRST-CLASS MAIL PERMIT NO. 48 JEFFERSON CITY, MO

POSTAGE WILL BE PAID BY ADDRESSEE

SCHOLASTIC
PO BOX 6114
JEFFERSON CITY MO 65102-9670

NO POSTAGE
NECESSARY IF
MAILED IN THE
UNITED STATES

BUSINESS REPLY MAIL

FIRST-CLASS MAIL PERMIT NO. 48 JEFFERSON CITY, MO

POSTAGE WILL BE PAID BY ADDRESSEE

SCHOLASTIC
PO BOX 6114
JEFFERSON CITY MO 65102-9670

N

Published by Scholastic Inc., 90 Old Sherman Turnpike, Danbury, Connecticut 06816.

ISBN 0-7172-6060-7

Printed in the U.S.A.
First printing, June 2003

SCHOLASTIC INC.
New York Toronto London Auckland Sydney
Mexico City New Delhi Hong Kong Buenos Aires

"C'mon, Dad!" Nemo called out. "It's time for school!"

The little clownfish Nemo was ready for his first day of school. One of Nemo's fins was smaller than the other, so he was not a great swimmer. Nemo, however, didn't let it slow him down.

But his father, Marlin, wasn't ready for Nemo to go. He was very protective of his son, and he worried—a lot.

“All right,” Marlin reluctantly agreed. Then he went over the safety rules.

“So . . . first we check to see that the coast is clear,” coached Marlin as he swam out of their anemone home. “We go out . . . and back in. And then we go out . . . and back in. And then—”

“Dad . . . ,” Nemo interrupted. He tugged on his father’s fin and pulled him out at last.

Soon Nemo and Marlin arrived at the school yard. The teacher Mr. Ray sailed in to take the children on a field trip.

"Bye, Dad!" Nemo shouted as Mr. Ray swam away.

"Bye, Son," Marlin called. "Be safe."

"You're doing pretty well," remarked one of the other fathers to Marlin. "I had a tough time when my oldest went out on the Drop-off."

Marlin gasped, "The Drop-off?!" The Drop-off was at the edge of the reef. There, a fish could swim right out into the open sea and right into danger.

Marlin immediately tried to catch up with the school group.

Meanwhile, Nemo and his new friends Tad, Sheldon, and Pearl sneaked away to look out over the edge of the Drop-off.

"I know what that is—a butt!" said Tad, pointing up at the bottom of a boat. Then Sheldon dared them to see who could swim closest to it.

Finally, it was Nemo's turn. "Come on, Nemo! How far can you go?" Tad challenged.

"Oh, um . . . my dad says it's not safe," Nemo said, not moving.

At that moment Marlin arrived. "You were about to swim into open water!" he accused. "You think you can do these things, but you just can't, Nemo."

Nemo was angry and embarrassed. As soon as his father turned his back, Nemo defiantly took off and swam all the way to the boat.

"Nemo! Get back here!" Marlin shouted. But it was too late. A diver appeared. He scooped up Nemo in a net, swam to the boat, and sped off.

Marlin couldn't swim fast enough to catch up with the boat. When he swam into a stream of fish to ask for help, he slammed into one of them.

"Sir? Are you okay?" asked the friendly blue fish. "Hi, I'm Dory."

"I have to find the boat!" said Marlin.

"Hey, I've seen a boat. Follow me!" she said.

Marlin followed Dory until she suddenly turned around and said, "Stop following me!"

Marlin was confused until Dory explained, "I suffer from short-term memory loss."

Marlin turned to leave and found himself facing a shark! Bruce the shark invited them to a "party" in a sunken submarine. The "party" was a meeting of sharks trying not to eat fish.

While there, Marlin spotted a diver's mask that had been dropped by Nemo's captor. Marlin hoped the writing on the mask could help him find his son.

"Ugh! What do these markings mean! I can't read human!" exclaimed Marlin.

"Well, we gotta find a fish that can!" encouraged Dory. They both grabbed the mask, which snapped and hit Dory in the face.

"Ow!" Dory cried, as blood trickled from her nose.

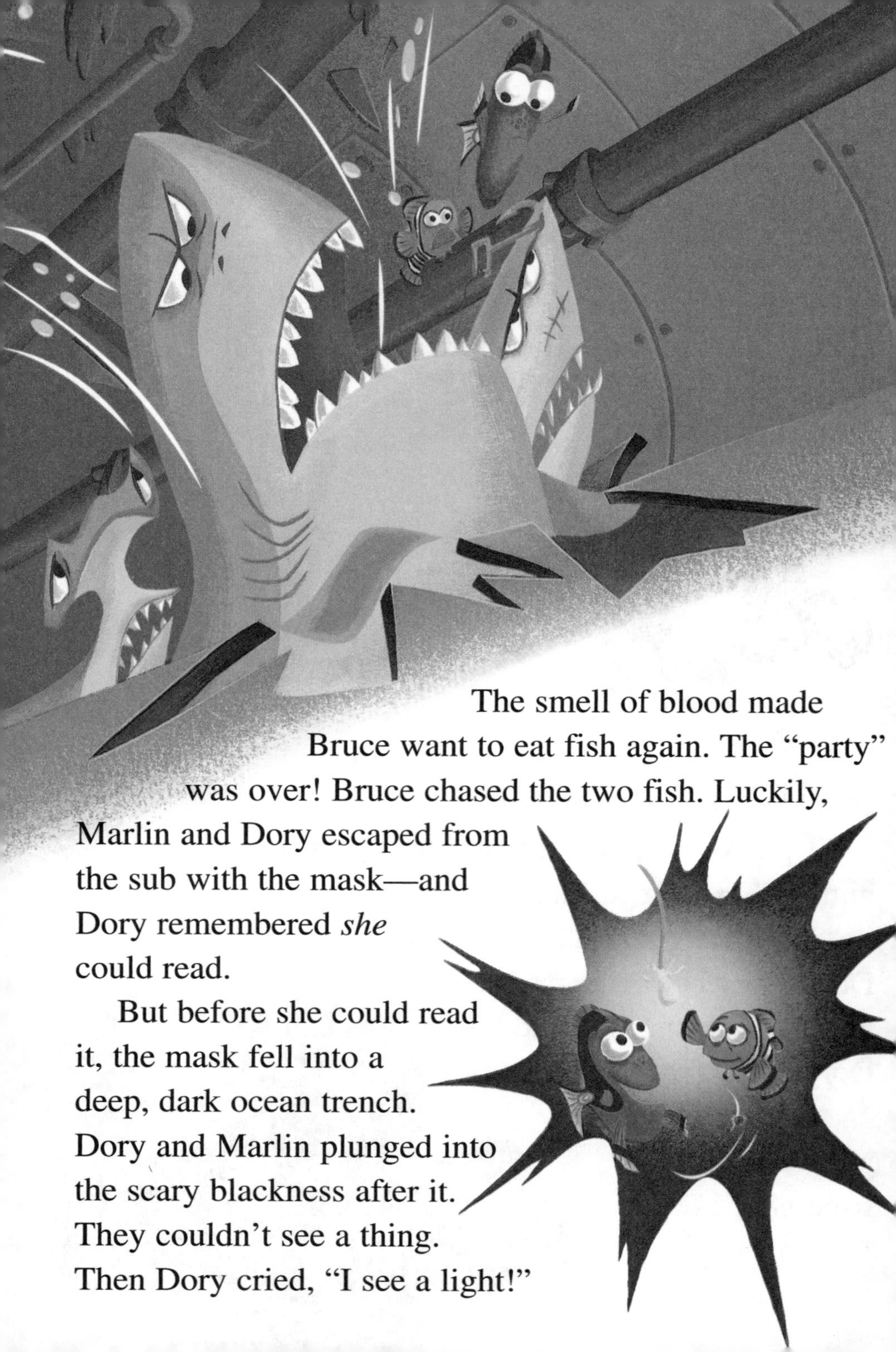

The smell of blood made Bruce want to eat fish again. The "party" was over! Bruce chased the two fish. Luckily, Marlin and Dory escaped from the sub with the mask—and Dory remembered *she* could read.

But before she could read it, the mask fell into a deep, dark ocean trench. Dory and Marlin plunged into the scary blackness after it. They couldn't see a thing. Then Dory cried, "I see a light!"

But the light turned out to be a hungry anglerfish's trap! The pair dodged the anglerfish's teeth just in time!

As the anglerfish chased them, its light fell on something. "Hey, look! A mask," Dory shouted.

"Read it!" Marlin ordered, trying to keep the anglerfish away from Dory.

"Bring him closer. I need the light," Dory answered.

Marlin led the anglerfish back and forth while Dory read the address on the mask. Then Dory and Marlin escaped in the nick of time!

"P. Sherman, 42 Wallaby Way, Sydney," said Dory proudly, as they swam off.

"Now where is that?" wondered Marlin.

It turned out that 42 Wallaby Way was a dentist's office in Sydney, Australia. The diver who had caught Nemo was the dentist, and he put the little fish into his office aquarium. The aquarium was home to an interesting group of fish known as the Tank Gang.

A friendly pelican named Nigel was perched on the dentist's windowsill visiting the Tank Gang. From them, Nemo found out that he was going to become a gift for the dentist's niece, Darla.

The Tank Gang told Nemo that the dentist had given Darla a fish last year, and it hadn't survived.

"I have to get back to my dad!" cried Nemo, horrified.

The leader of the Tank Gang, Gill, reassured Nemo that they would find a way to escape before Darla arrived.

Meanwhile back in the ocean . . . .

"P. Sherman, 42 Wallaby Way, Sydney!" Dory proudly repeated the address over and over.

Marlin asked a school of moonfish if they could tell him how to get to Sydney.

The moonfish didn't want to help Marlin, but they were happy to help Dory.

They formed themselves into an arrow pointing in the direction of Sydney.

"Great!" said Marlin, rushing off in the direction they had indicated.

"Oh, hey, ma'am?" the moonfish said to Dory. "When you come to the trench, swim through it—not over it."

"I'll remember!" said Dory, as she hurried to catch up with Marlin.

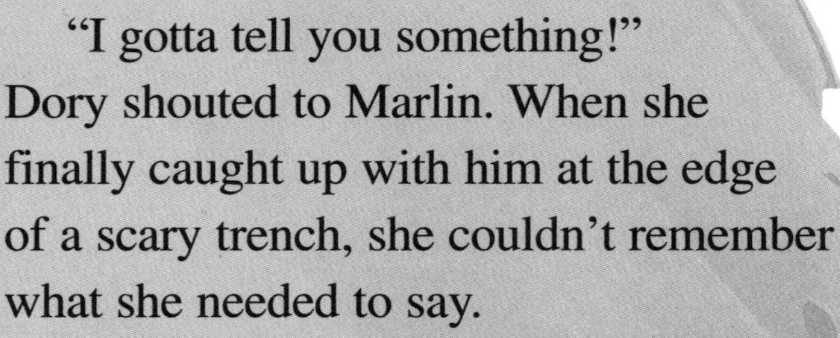

"I gotta tell you something!" Dory shouted to Marlin. When she finally caught up with him at the edge of a scary trench, she couldn't remember what she needed to say.

"We are going to swim over this thing," Marlin said.

"Something's telling me we should swim through it," said Dory. But Marlin easily tricked her into forgetting, and she happily followed him.

As it turned out, danger was lurking in the clear water above the trench. Dory was the first to find it.

"Ow!" Dory yelled. A baby jellyfish had stung her. Marlin rushed over and shooed the baby away.

"Let's be thankful this time it was just a little one," Marlin said. But then, when they looked around, Marlin and Dory discovered that they were surrounded by hundreds of jellyfish.

"This is bad," said Marlin.

But Dory was giggling. "Hey! Watch this!" she said, bouncing on the tops of the jellyfish.

Marlin quickly made up a game of jumping on the jellyfish tops. But there was one rule: "You can't touch the tentacles," Marlin explained.

The race began. After a while, Marlin hopped out of the jellyfish forest. But when he turned around, Dory was nowhere in sight.

"DORY!" Marlin cried. Then he saw her caught in a jellyfish's tentacles. Marlin swam back to his friend and dragged her out of the jellyfish forest. Then everything went black.

Later, Marlin woke to find that he was riding on the back of a sea turtle named Crush.

"Saw the whole thing, dude!" said Crush. He was quite impressed with Marlin's bravery. Marlin and Dory were in a group of sea turtles traveling on the East Australian Current, headed for Sydney. Marlin told the turtles about his quest to find Nemo.

The story passed quickly from sea creature to sea creature. Finally, Nigel, the pelican friend of the Tank Gang, heard about Marlin's search!

The ride on the current was great fun for Marlin and Dory, but suddenly Crush called out, "Get ready! Your exit's comin' up, man!"

"Thank you, dude-Crush!" Marlin shouted, as he and Dory left the current.

They soon found themselves in very murky water, looking for Sydney.

"Let's ask somebody for directions," suggested Dory, spotting what looked like a small fish far away. "There's somebody!"

"It's a fish we don't know. It could ingest us!" Marlin said nervously.

But Dory continued. “Woo-hoo! Little fellah?!” she called. But soon Marlin and Dory discovered that the “little fish” was a giant whale! In one big mouthful, it swallowed them both.

"We're in a whale!" shouted Marlin.

"Wow! A whale? You know, I speak whale." Dory listened carefully to the whale's loud moans. "He said we should go to the back of the throat."

Marlin was irritated. "Of course he wants us to go there. That's . . . eating us!"

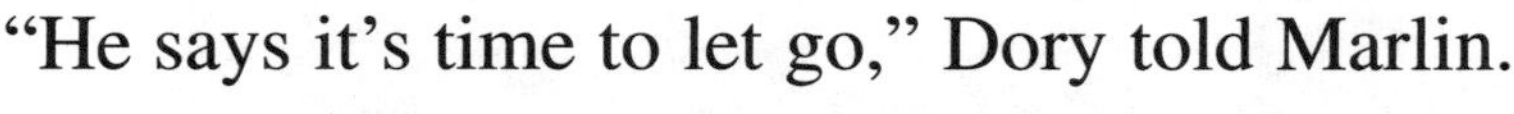

"He says it's time to let go," Dory told Marlin.

So Marlin let go. Suddenly he and Dory soon found themselves being shot out of the whale's spout. They flew into air, then splashed back into the sea.

When the two of them had recovered, they realized they were in Sydney Harbor.

"You were right, Dory. We made it! We're going to find my son!" cheered Marlin. "All we have to do is find the boat that took him."

But Sydney Harbor was full of boats. The two fish searched all through the night.

The next morning, a hungry pelican scooped the exhausted pair of fish into his beak, as he flew back towards land.

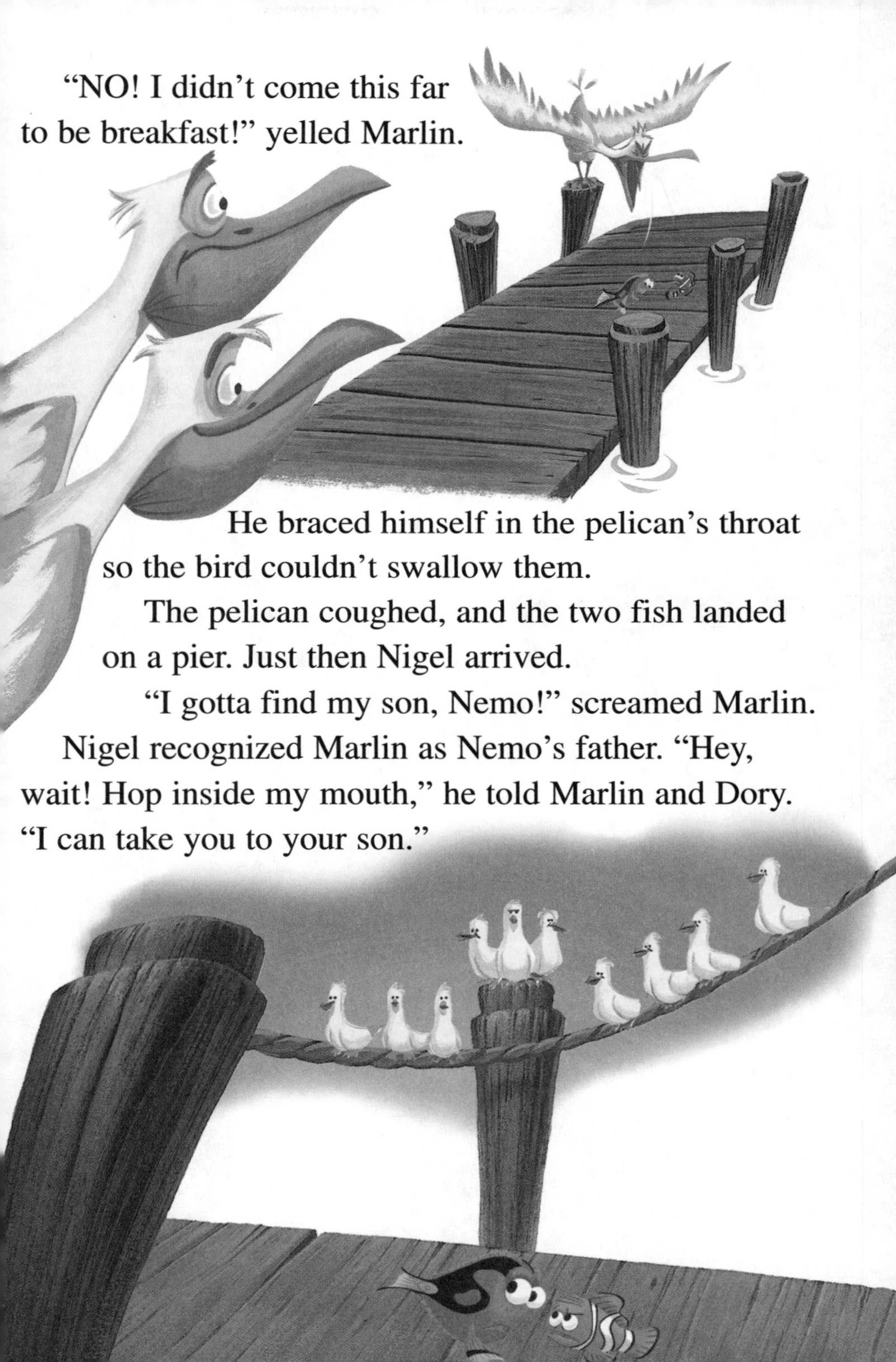

"NO! I didn't come this far to be breakfast!" yelled Marlin.

He braced himself in the pelican's throat so the bird couldn't swallow them.

The pelican coughed, and the two fish landed on a pier. Just then Nigel arrived.

"I gotta find my son, Nemo!" screamed Marlin.

Nigel recognized Marlin as Nemo's father. "Hey, wait! Hop inside my mouth," he told Marlin and Dory. "I can take you to your son."

Back at the dentist's office, things were going badly for little Nemo. Niece Darla was due to arrive any moment! The dentist had Nemo in a water-filled plastic bag, ready to give to her.

The dentist placed the bag with the panicked Nemo on a table.

The Tank Gang instructed Nemo to push the side of the bag so it would roll out of the open window. But just as Nemo succeeded in getting the bag rolling, the dentist noticed.

"Oh, that would be a nasty fall," the dentist said, catching the bag and setting it down on a tray. Suddenly the door to the office slammed open . . . and Darla stomped in!

But Nemo had an idea. He pretended to be dead, hoping that the dentist would flush him down the toilet. From there, Nemo planned to swim to the ocean.

"Hello, Darla, honey!" said the dentist to his niece.

"Oh no," he murmured when he noticed the motionless Nemo. The dentist quickly hid the bag behind his back, so Darla wouldn't see it.

Moments later the window burst open. In flew Nigel, carrying Dory and Marlin.

“What the—?” exclaimed the dentist when Nigel collided with him. The dentist dropped the bag holding Nemo onto a tray. A sharp instrument on the tray tore a small hole in the bag.

Then from his view in Nigel’s beak, Marlin spotted Nemo and thought his son was dead.

“Nemo!” he cried.

Nemo heard his father’s voice, but it was too late. The dentist had closed Nigel’s beak and shoved him out the window.

In the confusion, Darla had picked up the bag and swung it back and forth chanting, "Fishy! Fishy!"

Nemo poured out of the hole in the bag and became stranded on a dental tool.

The Tank Gang came to the rescue. With the help of his friends, Gill catapulted out of the tank, hit the dental tool with his tail, and launched Nemo through Darla's grabby hands into the spit sink!

Nemo disappeared down the drain.

"Don't worry!" Gill yelled to him. "All drains lead to the ocean!"

WOOOOSH!

Nemo swooped and swerved through the pipes. It was quite a ride!

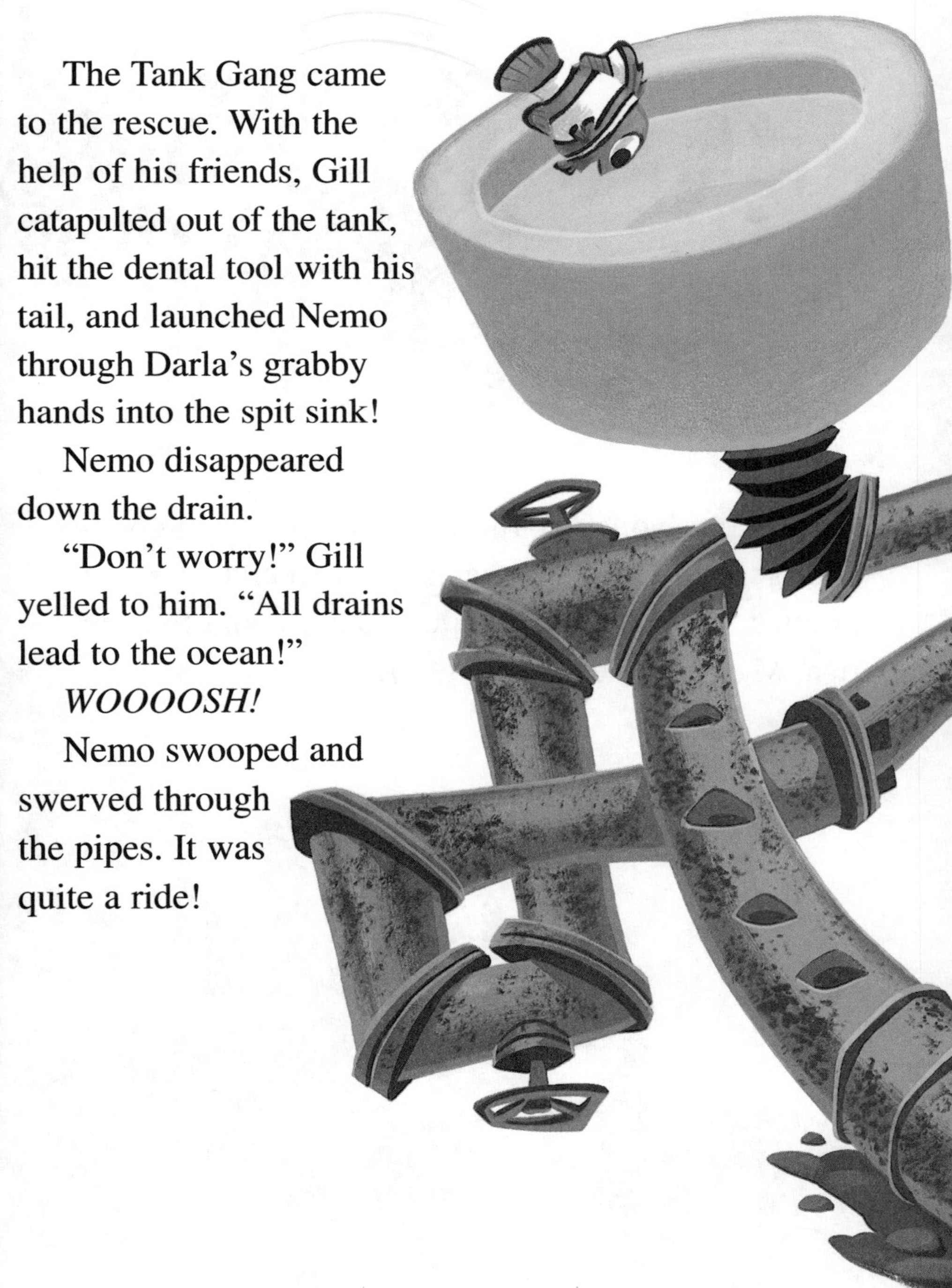

Back in Sydney Harbor, Marlin sadly said good-bye to Nigel and Dory. He swam past two crabs on a drainage pipe, and then he joined a school of grouper fish. Marlin started the long swim home.

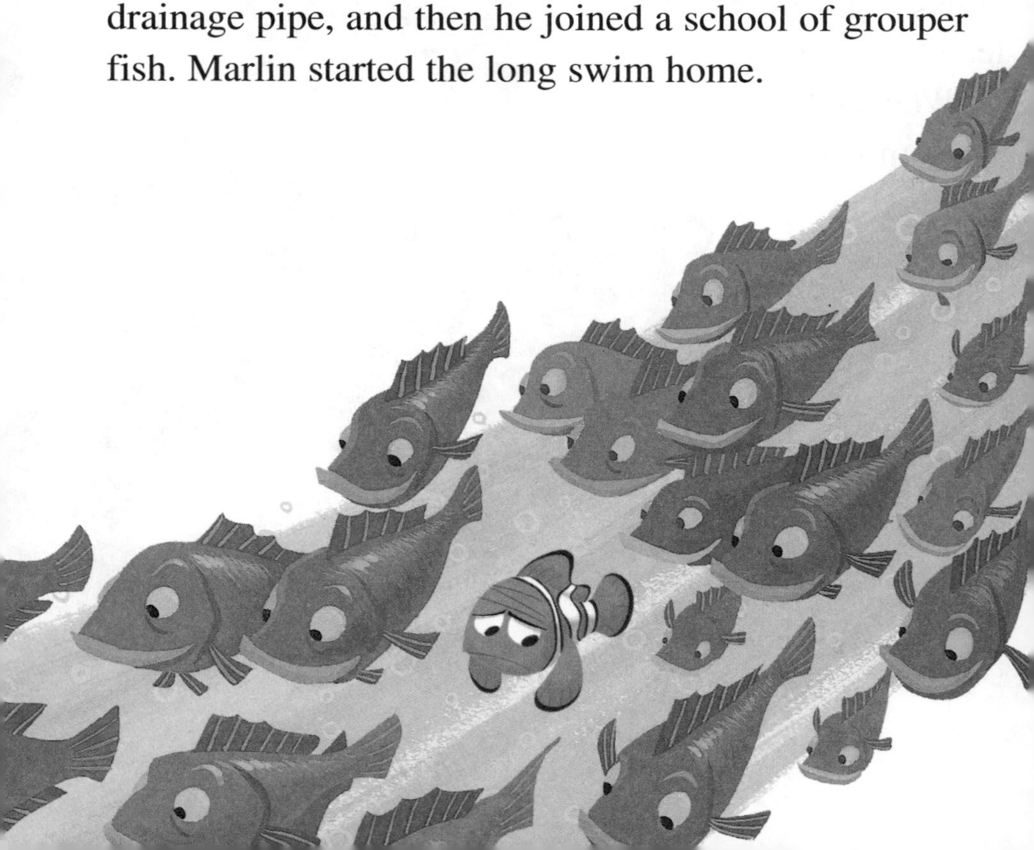

Nemo, meanwhile, ended his ride through the pipes of Sydney. He popped up through a hole next to the very same two crabs.

"Oi! Gotta live one here!" said one crab.

"Have you seen my dad?" Nemo asked. But he soon realized that the crabs were only interested in catching and eating him. So off Nemo swam—in the opposite direction that his father had gone.

Before long, Nemo found Dory swimming in circles and crying.

"I don't know where I am . . . I think I lost somebody, but I . . . need to remember . . . ."

"I'm Nemo," said the little fish. "I'm looking for someone, too."

"Nemo. That's a nice name," murmured Dory, not paying much attention. The two fish searched together for a while.

Suddenly Dory remembered! “NEMO!” She grabbed the little guy’s face tight with her fins. “You’re not dead! And your father . . . .”

“You know my father?” asked Nemo.

But Dory was already moving. “This way! Quick!”

Dory and Nemo swam over to the two crabs on the pipe and asked them whether they had seen Marlin.

"I'm not tellin'. And there's no way you're gonna make me," one of the crabs replied.

Dory was in no mood for his attitude. She grabbed the crab and thrust him above the water for the hungry seagulls to see. The crab quickly gave Dory and Nemo the directions they needed.

Nemo and Dory rushed to the fishing grounds to look for Marlin.

"Dad! Dad!" yelled Nemo, when he finally spotted Marlin in a crowd of grouper fish.

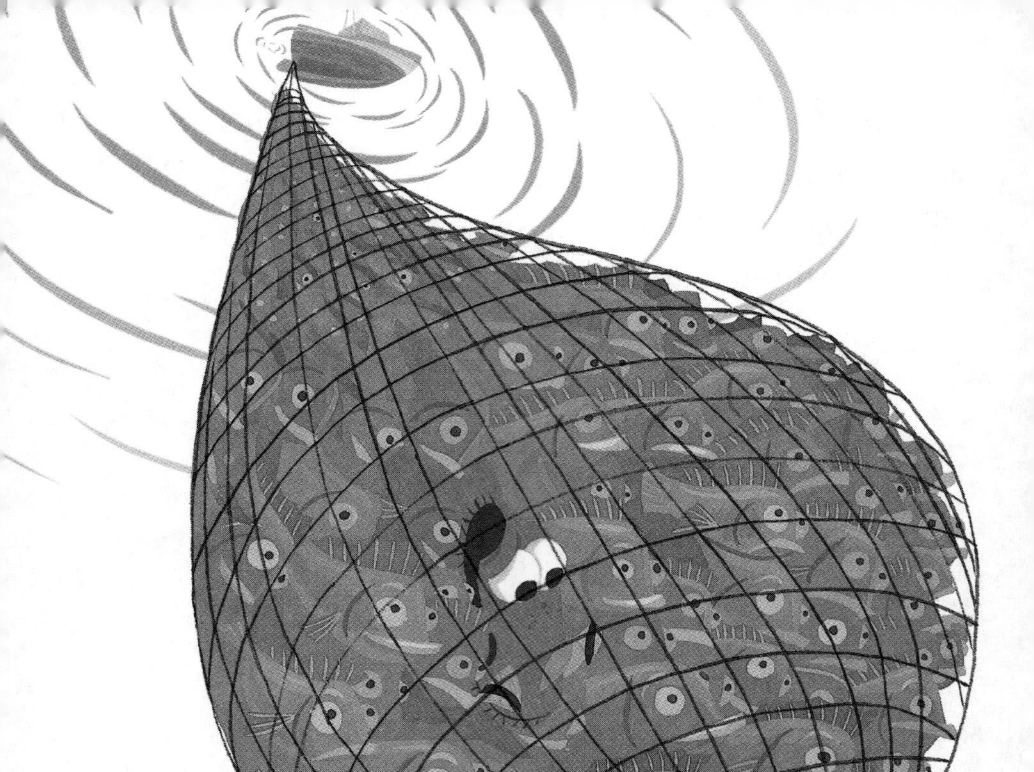

Marlin rushed to Nemo. Father and son were together at last!

"Look out!" yelled Dory as an enormous fishing net suddenly swept past them. The net missed Nemo and Marlin, but Dory and the grouper fish were caught.

"HEELLPP!!!" screamed Dory.

"Dad, I know what to do!" Nemo called, rushing to the rescue.

"No, no, no, no! Come back!" shouted Marlin. He didn't want to lose his son again.

"Dad," said Nemo, "I can do this!"

"I know you can," Marlin finally agreed, as Nemo swam into the net with the other fish.

Nemo urged the fish deep inside the net to swim to the bottom, while Marlin told those near the outside of the net to do the same. Together, Nemo and Marlin rallied the fish to swim together, causing the net to break loose. All the fish escaped, cheering. Nemo and Marlin were reunited.

Nemo and Marlin brought Dory back to their reef. Nemo started school again. He was overjoyed to be with his friends and Mr. Ray, the schoolteacher.

Just as Mr. Ray started to pull away, Nemo looked back at his dad. Then Nemo asked Mr. Ray to wait.

Nemo raced back and gave his dad a big hug. "Love ya, Dad," said Nemo.

"I love you, too, Son," said Marlin, holding tightly. "Now go have an adventure."